Greenwich Libraries
Book Sale

30p

JB 6 SEP 1979
A £2.450
J640

GREENWICH LIBRARIES
3 8028 00876101 4

HOME SWEET HOME

A HISTORY OF HOUSEWORK
ELEANOR ALLEN

ADAM & CHARLES BLACK · LONDON

Black's Junior Reference Books: General Editor R J Unstead

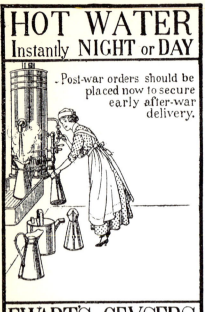

1	Houses	R J Unstead
2	Fish and the sea	Spike Noel
3	Travel by road	R J Unstead
4	The story of aircraft	Robert Hoare
5	Life before man	Duncan Forbes
6	Mining coal	John Davey
7	The story of the theatre	David Male
8	Stars and space	Patrick Moore
9	Monasteries	R J Unstead
10	Travel by sea	Robert Hoare
11	Cars	John Ray
12	Musical instruments	Denys Darlow
13	Arms and armour	Frederick Wilkinson
14	Farming in Britain	Frank Huggett
15	Law and order	John Dumpleton
16	Bicycles	Frederick Alderson
17	Heraldry	Rosemary Manning
18	Costume	Phillis Cunnington
19	The story of the post	Robert Page
20	Man in space	Henry Brinton
21	Castles	R J Unstead
22	Shops and markets	Paul White
23	Coins and tokens	Philip Leighton
24	Fairs and circuses	Paul White
25	Victorian children	Eleanor Allen
26	Food and cooking	Margaret Baker
27	Wartime children 1939–1945	Eleanor Allen
28	When the West was wild	Robert Hoare
29	Wash and brush up	Eleanor Allen
30	Getting about in towns	Paul White
31	Canal People	A J Pierce
32	The story of oil	Roger Piper
33	Home sweet home	Eleanor Allen

British Library Cataloguing in Publication Data

Allen, Eleanor
   Home sweet home.
   1. Home economics—Great Britain—History—
Juvenile literature
   I. Title
   640'.941   TX148

   ISBN 0-7136-1927-9

Published by A & C Black (Publishers) Limited, 35 Bedford Row, London WC1
First published 1979
ISBN 0 7136 1927 9
© A & C Black (Publishers) Limited

All rights reserved. No part of this publication may be reproduced, stored in a retrieval system, or transmitted, in any form or by any means, electronic, mechanical, photocopying, recording or otherwise, without prior permission in writing of A & C Black (Publishers) Limited.

Filmset and printed in Great Britain by
BAS Printers Limited, Over Wallop, Hampshire

Contents

		page			page
	Introduction	4	8	Cooking and kitchen equipment	46
1	Cleaning floors	5	9	Washing up	50
2	Dusting and polishing	17	10	Making clothes	54
3	Bed-making	22	11	Servantless homes	60
4	Lighting	28		Books for further reading	63
5	Making fires	33		Acknowledgments	63
6	Home decorating	36		Index	64
7	Preparing food	41			

Coping without electricity during the miners' strike of 1973–4

Toasting bread in front of an open fire

Introduction

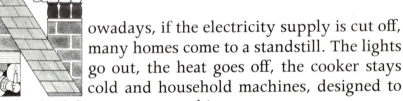

Nowadays, if the electricity supply is cut off, many homes come to a standstill. The lights go out, the heat goes off, the cooker stays cold and household machines, designed to make life easy, stop working.

But enterprising families aren't beaten. With their fire-places unblocked and an emergency bag of coal flickering into life, candles in saucers casting their calm yellow light and slices of bread dangling from old toasting forks, they sit back and delight in a romantic glimpse of home life as it once was, before everything went push-button easy.

Unfortunately, before they have time to reflect too deeply, there is a click and the stark reality of electric light jolts them back to the present.

But supposing we stay in the candle-light a little longer? Long enough to take a practical look at what running a home was really like, in the days when all the chores, from sweeping floors to candle-making and weaving cloth, were done by hand.

1 Cleaning floors

Cleaning floors is still reckoned a hard chore. Yet we have vacuum-cleaners, electric floor-polishers and many types of easy-to-care-for covers. In the past, people had little or no choice of covers and no machines to help them. How, then, did they manage?

Inside a peasant's cottage. People often had to cook, eat and sleep in a single room

Earth, stone and rushes

In the Middle Ages people's biggest concern was not how to keep their floors clean, but how to make them less damp and chill.

A peasant's house had no proper flooring at all – just cold damp earth. The only treatment it received was a thorough beating to make the surface hard and smooth and, sometimes, a sprinkling of bullocks' blood. Sprinkling blood sounds gruesome and unhygienic, but when the floor was dry the surface was much harder and shinier.

To keep out the cold a peasant's wife covered her earth floor with a layer of loose rushes, or maybe straw.

On the whole rushes were more convenient. They were warm underfoot and were easy to find along the banks of a stream. If the housewife picked her own they cost her nothing.

But loose rushes had one big disadvantage: there was no way of cleaning them. The whole lot had to be cleared out and renewed. It was a big job and so the housewife didn't usually do it more than once or twice a year. Occasionally she strewed a few fresh rushes on top, but usually the rushes lay undisturbed month in and month out, absorbing all the grease and filth of the household and harbouring fleas and other pests. Eventually they became so foul that on hot days they gave off a vile smell and a vapour rose from them.

In the castles and large houses of the Middle Ages the floors were made of wood or stone. But they too could be cold and damp. So, like the peasants, the lords and their retainers sought warmth from rushes. A servant was made responsible for changing them, but with dozens of retainers as well as dogs and other animals sleeping, living and eating together in the great hall, the lords' floors must have been just as filthy as the peasants'.

Even in wealthy homes in Tudor times, loose rushes mixed with clippings of herbs were often still in use. Trodden herbs gave off a fragrant smell and Queen Elizabeth herself had her floors strewn with them.

For her palace at Greenwich, Elizabeth chose a covering of bay leaves. Presumably her floor coverings were changed often enough to keep them fresh. But most people were just as slovenly as they had been in the Middle Ages. The state of English floors so appalled Erasmus, a Dutch scholar who visited England in the sixteenth century, that he wrote this description of them in a letter

Popular herbs for strewing
Basil, bay, daisies, lavender, majoram, rosemary and sage.

> The floors . . . are covered with rushes which are now and then renewed, but not so as to disturb the foundation which sometimes remains for twenty years nursing a collection of spittle, vomits, excrement of dogs and human beings, spilt beer and fish bones and other filth . . . .

No wonder he suspected them of being responsible for outbreaks of plague!

Elizabethan rooms were sometimes spread with straw, instead of rushes, to keep out the cold and damp

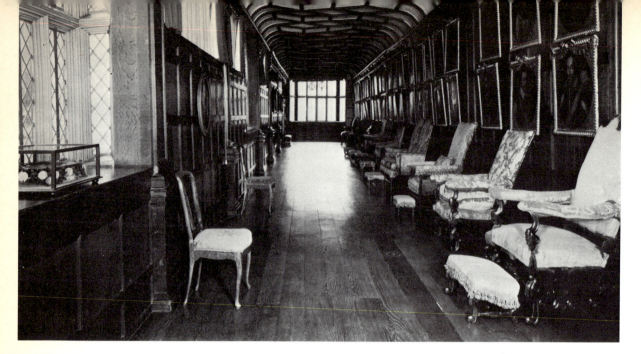

Highly polished wooden floorboards at Knole in Kent

A maidservant with her broom

Rush matting

Plaited rushes made into mats began to be used in some houses from Tudor times. These were much more hygienic, because they could be swept and occasionally lifted up so that the floor underneath could be cleaned. But they never entirely took the place of loose rushes because they were more costly. In 1603 rush matting cost about 5p a square metre – quite a lot when a year's wages might not amount to more than £2.00.

Well into the eighteenth century loose rushes continued to be the normal covering for cottage floors, and even quite rich people thought them good enough for the children's and servants' rooms.

Wooden floors

When standards of living improved in the seventeenth and eighteenth centuries it became the fashion in rich and middle-class houses to have floors of polished wood. These were usually of oak, scattered with a small rug or two and later partly covered by a carpet square.

A lot of information on eighteenth-century methods of floor cleaning can be found in books of instructions written for household servants. Very similar methods were still being recommended in the nineteenth century.

Wet-scouring

This must have been a very unpopular job, particularly in the middle of winter. There were a number of theories about what materials should be used, but generally housemaids were equipped with large wooden pails of cold water, bowls of sand, and hard scrubbing brushes. The maids had to go down on hands and knees and work their way across the floors, scrubbing the boards with the sand and cold water and afterwards rinsing them with a flannel. All the windows were flung wide open to allow the floors to dry.

Dry-rubbing

Wet-scouring was tremendously hard work, but the polishing which followed – dry-rubbing as it was known – was even harder. The housemaids exchanged their scrubbing brushes for long-handled brooms with large heads about 30 centimetres long and 20 centimetres wide. They sprinkled the floors with handfuls of hot, dry white sand and brushed it back and forth with heavy-headed brooms until the boards were smooth and shiny again. Anyone who has ever smoothed off a piece of wood with sandpaper will realise how long it must have taken to do a whole floor.

In gallant France this method of polishing was thought too hard for women, so there it was done by the men servants. Instead of using a broom they fastened a brush to one of their feet and polished with great style – a sort of sand-dance!

In scouring boards a little mason's dust answers just as well as soap and is a vast deal cheaper.

Use as little soap as possible. Fuller's earth and fine sand preserves the colour of the boards and does not leave a white appearance as soap does.

Hints on wet-scouring
To prevent scouring turning oak boards a dirty, dull white colour, wash them over after scouring with water coloured with umber and yellow ochre.

Tea leaves must not be mouldy or they will impart no pleasant freshness to the room, nor dried or they are useless in catching dust.

To make brushes and mops
A very good and durable mop may be made with cuttings, which are sold cheap, by blanket manufacturers.

When you take a walk in summer it is no trouble to bring home a few handfuls of heather. When they have slowly dried you can bind them up into small bundles with a bit of waxed thread.

Sweeping

Between scourings, which varied in frequency from about once a fortnight to once or twice a year, the maids swept the floors with 'common hair' brooms. There was a skill in sweeping polished floors. If a maid was clumsy and wielded her broom too vigorously she caused the dust to rise in clouds and settle round the room. The dust had to be rolled gently along the floor and into the dust-pan.

Before starting to sweep, it was thought wise to close all the doors and windows and cover the furniture with dust sheets. Though it sounds an odd idea, sprinkling handfuls of moist tea-leaves over the floor was recommended as a good way to lay the dust before sweeping. They also left a pleasant fragrance in the room. But the maid had to be careful to sweep them all up with the dust.

Cleaning materials

Cleaning equipment was quite expensive. The price of an ordinary broom rose from between 2½p and 5p in the seventeenth century to between 15p and 20p in the nineteenth – a big slice out of a week's wages in those days. Cottage housewives were advised to save money by using a handful of straw for scrubbing and making their own brushes and mops.

A floor brush of the 1920s

Carpets

Have you ever walked round a stately home and been shown carpets 200 years old or more? They might well have seemed in better condition than some of your own carpets at home after only two or three years' wear.

In the past carpets were such tremendous luxuries that their owners lavished far more care and protection on them than we would ever think of doing.

The first rugs and carpets in England were imported from the East after the Crusades by kings and nobles. But they were so valuable they were used to cover chests or tables, or hung on the walls from 'tenterhooks'. No one dreamed of walking on them.

Small rugs or 'fote' (foot) carpets began to appear on polished floors in the seventeenth century when standards of living improved, but it wasn't until the eighteenth century that carpets became fairly plentiful. Even then they were only to be found in the best rooms of the rich.

The Queen Elizabeth Room at Penshurst Place in Kent. The carpet is over 100 years old

A magnificent marble hallway. In the 18th century rich people liked to impress visitors with floors of patterned marble. Carpets became less fashionable

A good idea of how much care and protection carpets received is given in a housekeeping book written in 1776 by Mrs Suzanna Whatman of Turkey Court in Kent. She recommended beating and brushing the carpet, then scouring it with ox-gall, soap, and warm water.

In Mrs Whatman's day carpets were not as colour-fast or fade-proof as they are now, so protecting them was usually considered the best way of caring for them. For much of the time they were kept concealed beneath baize covers or linen 'druggets', which were only removed if the room was being used. In many homes carpets were taken up for the summer months and stored in an attic away from harmful dust and sunshine.

When carpets were actually in use the maid had to sprinkle those in the best rooms with tea leaves before she swept them because tea leaves were supposed to preserve the colours. When a fire was lit she had to turn back the ends of the carpets nearest the fireplace each day and sweep underneath in case any coal dust or ash had fallen there. From time to time she turned the carpets over completely and left them face down for people to walk over them. That, claimed Mrs Whatman, 'gets out the dust much better than beating them'.

Even by the middle of the nineteenth century, carpets were still such expensive items that they were carefully cherished. The appearance of the sun could throw owners of new carpets into a panic. Mary Smith, a character in Mrs Gaskell's novel *Cranford*, writes:

> The greatest event was that Miss Jenkyns had purchased a new carpet for the drawing-room. Oh, the busy time Miss Matty and I had in chasing the sunbeams as they fell in an afternoon right down on this carpet through the blind-less window! We spread newspapers over the places . . . and lo! in a quarter of an hour the sun had moved and was blazing away on a fresh spot; down again we went on our knees to alter the position of the newspapers.

Carpet-sweepers replaced brooms at the end of the 19th century

When the same Miss Jenkyns gives a party, Mary describes how she and Miss Matty spent a whole morning stitching together pieces of newspaper to form little paths to every chair put out for visitors 'lest their shoes might dirty or defile the purity of the carpet!'

Oil floor-cloths and foot-scrapers

In the middle of the eighteenth century some people began to use a new type of floor covering known as 'oil floor-cloths' to cover bare boards. But it did not make floor cleaning any simpler. Unlike modern floor-cloth, or linoleum, it needed more than just a wipe with a damp mop. It had to be cleaned with milk and polished until it was dry. Once a week it had to be turned over, otherwise the sides curled up.

Floors in the entrance halls of wealthy houses were often marble in the eighteenth century, or of ceramic tiles in the nineteenth, yet even these must have been difficult to keep clean when the road outside was unpaved and littered with horse dung.

Visitors trampled up the front steps from the street in shoes caked with mud and filth, then paused outside the door in a polite attempt to remove the worst of it with the aid of a foot-scraper. You can still see them outside older houses.

A poor man's foot-scraper
A scraper at the door might be made with a bit of iron hoop lodged into two strong sticks, split a little way down and fixed into the earth.

A foot-scraper

Before breakfast every morning the unfortunate maid had to emerge on to the front steps with her pail of water and scrub away all the accumulation of dirt from the day before.

In later Victorian times carpets became cheaper and some people began to have them covering the whole floor. But even a big expanse of carpet was still swept with brooms – a common hair broom for daily care and a whisk brush made from tough grass for a thorough going-over once a week. Stairs which had previously been left bare and echoing began to be carpeted too. They were brushed down with a short-haired brush called a 'drugget brush'.

The vacuum-cleaner

This tremendous aid to floor cleaning took around forty years to become popular!

In fact it's not so surprising. The early models of about 1905 cost a lot of money for those days – between £12 and £15 – and they were not easy to use. They were very cumbersome and had to be worked by hand, not electricity. One machine needed two people to work it, the first to push it along, the second to turn the handle.

Electric machines costing about £35 could be bought a few years later.

One of the first vacuum-cleaners

Vacuum-cleaning was thought such hard work that rich households often employed outside contractors to do the work

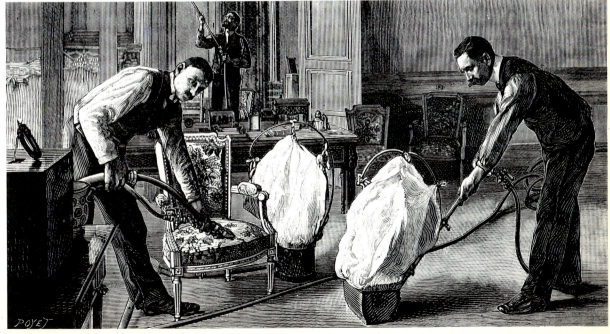

Yet *another* vacuum-cleaner salesman!

An early electric floor-polisher

Yet although available, few people who could afford them were interested in buying them. There were still plenty of servants who were cheap to employ, and who could do the job perfectly well using a 40p broom or a patent carpet sweeper for about 80p. No mistress was prepared to buy an expensive machine just to save her servants hard work!

After the First World War servants were more difficult to find. More and more well-off women found that for the first time in their lives they had to handle a dust-pan and broom. Suddenly the idea of owning a vacuum-cleaner became attractive.

Working-class housewives were attracted by vacuum-cleaners too, but they could not afford them. Nor did they have the mains electricity needed to run them until the 1940s and early 1950s. Once vacuum-cleaners were within the reach of everyone, however, sales rocketed. Selling techniques helped a lot. Armies of notoriously persuasive salesmen sold them over the doorstep, with tempting offers of free demonstrations and 'easy terms' which few housewives could resist.

2 Dusting and polishing

The state dining-room at Nostell Priory. The furniture was designed by Chippendale and carved from mahogany

Dusting and polishing weren't an important part of housework until the eighteenth century. Until then there was very little furniture and few ornaments to dust and polish, even in wealthy homes. In poorer homes the furniture, often no more than a wooden stool or two and a table, was usually solid and home-made. In better-off homes furniture was handsomer, and had often been handed down from generation to generation.

It was in the eighteenth century that well-to-do people felt the need to have more furniture, ornaments, paintings and mirrors about them. Then there was more dusting and polishing to be done, but still not as much as you might expect because the furniture spent a lot of time hidden beneath dust sheets. Each piece was hand-carved and so expensive that owners protected it well by having the maids cover it whenever a room wasn't in constant use.

With a pair of bellows blow the dust off your Pictures and Frames for you must not touch a Picture with a Brush of any sort.

17

Thomas Chippendale, one of the most famous furniture designers of the eighteenth century, supplied dust covers made of calico with all his furniture. He even went so far as to supply soft leather stockings for any that had gilt legs!

The favourite wood for furniture in the eighteenth century was mahogany. Sometimes it was intricately carved. At Turkey Court, Mrs Whatman instructed her maid to use a painter's brush to dust out the carvings on her mahogany sideboards.

Other pieces of furniture were made of cheaper woods which were painted a light colour to harmonize with the walls, or else lacquered in black or green and decorated with gilt. These had to be handled very carefully when they were dusted, for they were easily chipped.

Mrs Whatman was fortunate enough to be able to afford slatted blinds called 'Venetian blinds' to protect her carpets and furniture. These had just

A laquered cabinet on an ornate gilt stand

come into use in England. At Turkey Court a shaft of sunlight in a room was a signal for instant action. The maid was issued with a timetable showing when the sun reached each important room, and she had strict instructions to run round the house ahead of it, snapping down the blinds. If a sly beam found a chink in the blinds, Mrs Whatman felt obliged to 'shut the shudders' (shutters).

By the 1840s machine-made furniture was starting to replace hand-made furniture. This meant that more could be produced and, because the price went down, more people could buy it. It became the fashion to cram into the house as much furniture as possible – large mahogany tables, carved bookcases, needle-work tables, stands called 'whatnots' for displaying things and often, given pride of place, a piano. Everything had to be kept well dusted and polished, and that wasn't easy with grime given off by coal fires and candle, oil or gas lighting.

Commercially produced furniture polish was a help to Victorian maids

The Victorians had a passion for ornaments and decorations of all kinds

One of the many window-cleaning devices that came onto the market during the 1830s

Is it possible that any lady will see her servant thus exposed, and let her run the risk of being killed, when a remedy can be had for the small sum of 7s. 6d. ?

A good furniture polish
To one pint of linseed oil, by a gentle heat, melt together two ounces of yellow resin, eighteen ounces of beeswax, and two ounces of borage-root.

Furniture polish was usually made at home and mixing it was yet another chore for the busy servants. Housekeeping books and ladies' magazines in their 'Things Worth Knowing' sections, gave recipes and tips on how to make it.

The Victorians were also fond of collecting knick-knacks such as shell-boxes, clocks, ornaments, photographs and vases and standing them on mantelpieces and tables. They hung pictures and mirrors in gilt frames from the walls and displayed china in glass-fronted cabinets. All these trapped dirt and fluff. Fashionable collections of wax fruit and stuffed birds would have been impossible to dust, so they had special glass domes to protect them.

No wonder the Victorians also shrouded their furnishings in dust sheets whenever they could. Mrs Gaskell, in her book *North and South*, calls this custom 'bagging-up'. One drawing-room she describes looked as though 'no one had been in it since the day when the furniture was bagged-up with as much care as if the house was to be overwhelmed with lava and discovered a thousand years hence'.

Bagging-up persisted until fairly modern times. Even working-class families kept their front parlour under dust sheets and only used it on very special occasions like Christmas, weddings and funerals.

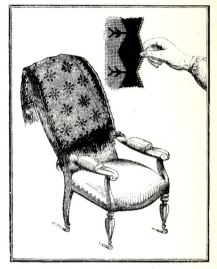

Macassar oil became very popular among fashion-conscious Victorian men

When furniture was in use, the Victorians still had methods of protecting it. Tables were guarded from dust and scratches by being draped with thick cloths fringed with bobbles. Upholstered settees and chairs had loose covers made in a flowered cotton material called 'chintz', which was easy to launder.

When men started wearing an oily preparation called 'Macassar Oil' on their hair, women took to draping the backs of their chairs and settees with white cloths crocheted along the edges which were called, appropriately, 'anti-macassars'. This fashion has lingered on and there are still some in use, even though hair oil is no longer in fashion and most upholstery materials can be cleaned.

Window-cleaning

From time to time housemaids had to dust window-frames with a painter's brush and clean the windows, inside and out. To clean sash windows on the outside, housemaids were sometimes expected to climb out and balance precariously on narrow ledges several floors up. Not surprisingly, there were reports of maids losing their balance and falling to their deaths. Such accidents caused public outcries in Victorian times.

Manufacturers were of course quick to cash in on such protests. Window-cleaning contraptions, which would wash both inside and outside at once, sound like a good idea, but obviously they didn't work, for they never caught on. A man with a bucket, washleather and ladder was found to be the most efficient way of cleaning windows. He still is, though manufacturers continue to search for the perfect window-cleaning gadget.

How to make an anti-macassar

Cleaning windows the traditional way

3 Bed-making

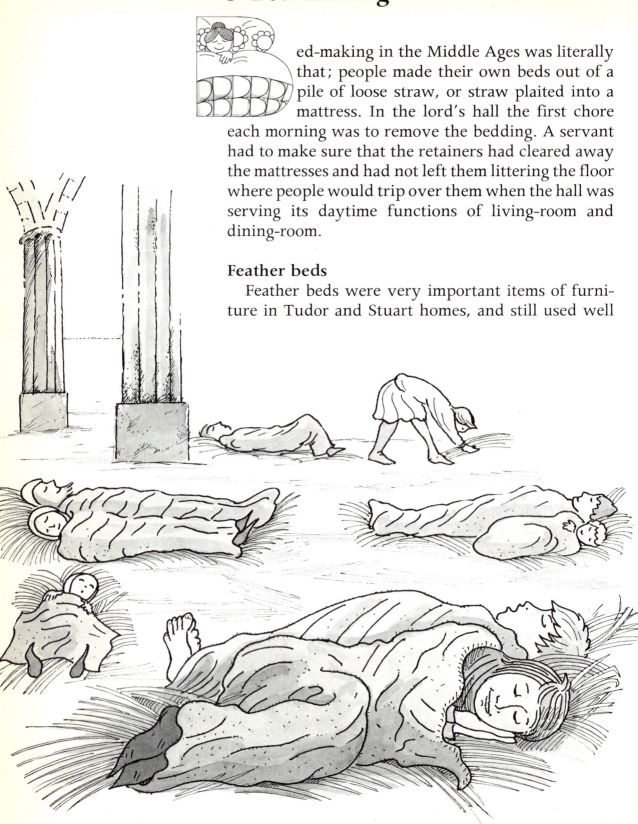

Bed-making in the Middle Ages was literally that; people made their own beds out of a pile of loose straw, or straw plaited into a mattress. In the lord's hall the first chore each morning was to remove the bedding. A servant had to make sure that the retainers had cleared away the mattresses and had not left them littering the floor where people would trip over them when the hall was serving its daytime functions of living-room and dining-room.

Feather beds

Feather beds were very important items of furniture in Tudor and Stuart homes, and still used well into the nineteenth century. In those days if a farmer's or merchant's wife wanted a feather bed she didn't buy one – she made her own. The family hens provided the stuffing, for even town-dwellers kept a few hens in their backyards.

Making a feather bed must have needed a lot of patience and determination. Twenty pounds or more of feathers had to be collected and saved in a large tub – an enormous quantity when one thinks of how much a feather weighs.

Before they could be used, the feathers had to be cleaned. Houses didn't have running water so the housewife had to carry them to a stream and do the unpleasant job there. Humping home a large bag of wet feathers can't have been very agreeable either.

She then spread out the feathers to dry in the bread oven while it was still hot from making bread.

The largest carved oak four-poster bed in the world. It is known as the Great Bed of Ware

A dozen or more hens would have to be plucked to make a single feather pillow

Later she hung the feathers in the chimney in a bag and left them to be 'cured' by smoke. After they had been cured they were ready to stuff into a mattress cover. She would have spent many hours making that herself too.

This method of making feather mattresses and pillows was used until Victorian times. One nineteenth-century writer claimed to have known young women who saved all the feathers of the fowl they plucked while working as kitchen maids in the houses of the rich. By the time they were married they had saved enough to make a mattress, bolster and pillows. Nowadays we should think a pile of feathers a strange item for a 'bottom drawer'!

Feather mattresses for beds in wealthy homes were made by professional upholsterers. From the sixteenth century through to the second half of the nineteenth century, the beds themselves were enormously large four-posters, hung with elaborate curtains and covers in rich materials. The thick hangings shut out draughts in the large unheated rooms. But although they were both useful and beautiful, they were also very impractical because they weren't easy to clean.

Dust-laden hangings smelt suffocatingly musty when they were closed for the night, and drawing them must have caused a lot of bed-time sneezing! At Turkey Court Mrs Whatman's method of protecting the tops of the bed canopies was to spread sheets of paper over them. Twice a year the maid had to lift the papers down and replace them.

Dusty hangings were a nuisance, but bed-bugs must have been sheer torture. Everybody had them. Even in the most wealthy and elegant homes they crept out each night to disturb sleepers in their sumptuous beds. Trying to get rid of them was a constant problem and it was discussed quite unashamedly in the politest ladies' journals and housekeeping books.

Bug-infested mattresses and pillows were not easy to deal with. Usually the housewife or her servants went through the tiresome task of unpicking them once a year on a fine day and spreading the feathers out in the sun in the hope that exposure would drive the pests away.

Bed-posts had to be sponged over regularly with one of the many concoctions recommended, most of which contained camphor. All had to be mixed at home and they must have been both messy to apply and sometimes obnoxious to sleep with.

To destroy bugs
Mix $\frac{1}{2}$ a pint of spirits of turpentine and $\frac{1}{2}$ a pint of best rectified spirits of wine in a strong bottle; add, in small pieces, $\frac{1}{2}$oz of camphor. Shake the mixture well, and, with a sponge or a brush, wet the infected parts. The dust should be well brushed from the bedstead and furniture, to prevent any stain. If this precaution be taken, there will be no danger of soiling the richest damask. The smell of the mixture will soon evaporate after using. Only one caution is necessary: never apply the mixture by candlelight, lest the spirits should catch the flame of the candle and set the bed-curtains on fire.

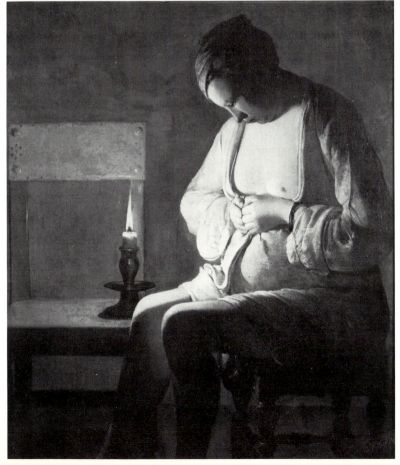

Painting of a woman squashing a flea

When brass bedsteads came into fashion they were designed with bulbous bases over the castors in an attempt to prevent bugs from climbing up the legs. The castors themselves were sometimes placed in small cups of camphor or paraffin.

In Victorian times bed-making was not the casual affair it is these days. All the windows were flung open and the bed-clothes were stripped off and placed over a clothes horse or the back of a chair to air. Then the mattresses were arranged to suit 'the fancy of the occupant'. As Mrs Beeton explains in her famous *Book of Household Management*,

Another method of killing bugs
After cleaning the bedstead thoroughly, rub it over with hog's lard. The lard should be rubbed on with a woollen cloth. Bugs will not infest such a bedstead for a whole season. The reason for this is the antipathy of insects for grease of any kind. *(This recipe was surely likely to deter sleepers as well as bugs!)*

> Some like beds sloping from the top towards the feet, swelling slightly in the middle; others perfectly flat; a good housemaid will accommodate each bed to the taste of the sleeper, taking care to shake, beat and turn it well in the process.

If any feathers escaped from the mattress or pillows in the shaking they had to be pushed back through the seam. Any bits of fluff which fell onto the carpet had to be swept up with a dust-pan and brush.

Apart from making beds there was an emptying job to do in the bedrooms. Chamber pots had to be dragged out every morning from under the bed and emptied into slop-buckets; dirty water from the hand basins had to be swilled away and any unused water left in the water jug had to be poured out.

A brass bedstead. Note the handle for adjusting the tension of the mattress

Bed-warming

Removing the winter chill from sheets was not an easy job in the days before central heating and electric blankets. Nowadays, when we see warming-pans hanging on walls simply as decorations, we tend to forget that they were once actually used. Weary housewives or maids, armed with a pair of tongs, had to fill them with hot embers from the kitchen fire, carry them carefully to the bedrooms and smooth them back and forth across the sheets.

In Victorian times stone hot-water bottles took over from warming-pans. Water had to be boiled to fill them and they were carried upstairs wrapped in a woollen cloth. It was essential to put the stopper in carefully, otherwise the sleeper could be scalded, or wake up shivering in a cold damp bed.

Some families, instead of a hot water-bottle, wrapped the hot-plate out of the oven in a piece of old sheeting, or heated up a brick in the oven and warmed their feet on that. Despite electric blankets and duvets, many people still cling to the comfort of a rubber hot water-bottle.

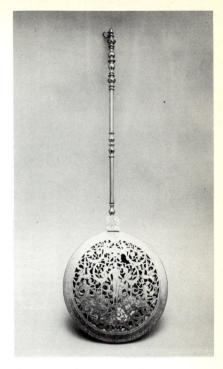

An ornate brass warming pan made in 1602

A 1929 advertisement for an electric blanket

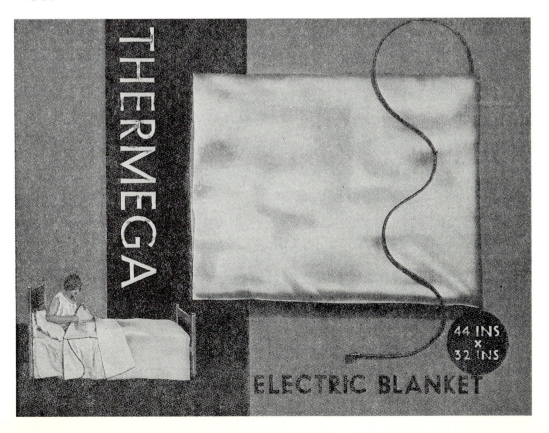

4 Lighting

Today, when it begins to get dark, we click on a switch or two and the room can seem as bright as day. All we need to do to keep it so is change the light bulbs occasionally and remember to pay our electricity bills.

In the past, lighting a house was a dreadful problem. Candles, oil lamps and gas jets not only gave off soot and fumes which made the furnishings and decorations dirty, they all needed a lot of attention. Housewives often had to make their own candles, so that light after nightfall depended on their efficiency.

Candle-making

Dark yellowish-coloured tallow candles were the most common for everyday use. They were made out of animal fats, usually mutton. Whenever the family ate meat the housewife saved left-over fat and put it aside until she had enough for candle-making. She melted the fat, dipped the wicks into it and let them dry, then repeated the process until the candles had built up to the required thickness.

Welsh women making candles

Candles were made of dried rushes dipped in fat. The candlestick consisted of a rough stick set upright in a circular stand. A forked twig held the candle in place

Standing over a pot of hot rancid fat was a smelly job. The smell must have got into her hair and clothes and pervaded the house. No wonder many wives handed over their fat to a candle-maker and paid him to do the job for them.

Country housewives made their lights out of rushes dipped in fat, which worked out a lot cheaper. In summer the old women and children of a village gathered the rushes from the banks of streams. Before they were ready for use they had to be soaked in water, then laid out on the grass to be dried and bleached by the sun.

A housewife could buy one kilogram of prepared rushes for $12\frac{1}{2}$p and there were about 4,000 rushes to a kilogram – an awful lot of dipping if she used them all. 'The careful wife', we are told, 'obtains all her fat for nothing, for she saves the scummings of her bacon pot for this use.'

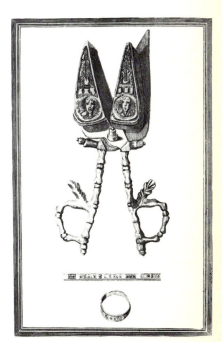

A pair of snuffers

Various kinds of oil lamps popular in the 1890s

To remove grease stains from floor boards
Take ½lb of fuller's earth and ¼lb of pearlash; make them into a paste with about a quart of boiling water; spread a thick coating of this over the grease stains and leave it for ten or twelve hours.

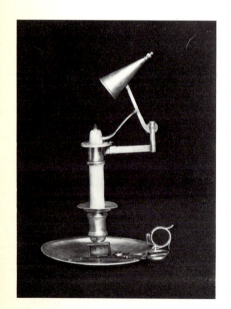

A candlestick with an automatic extinguisher. A pair of snuffers rests on the stand

But it took a long time. About 2¼ kilograms were needed to dip just under half a kilogram of rushes. By making her own rush lights it was estimated that a housewife could provide her family with 800 hours of light for 15p – five times as many than if she used tallow candles.

Good quality wax candles had to be bought and only the wealthy could afford these. In the eighteenth century they cost about 6½p each.

But whichever type of candle was used, it needed careful attention. The charred ends of wicks had to be snipped off constantly with a pair of 'snuffers' to stop them curling over into the melted wax and putting the flame out. In large houses this job kept several servants fully occupied all evening.

Melted wax or fat had to be scraped off the candlesticks and often off the furniture and floors. Rush lights had to be burnt at an angle, so there was no really effective way of preventing them from scattering drops of grease. Guttering candles being carried about the house left a trail of grease spots too, especially if they were being carried carelessly. Mrs Whatman's floors must have suffered because she insisted that the most important thing a servant could be taught was how to carry her candle upright.

A gaselier. Gas lighting became popular in the Victorian era

Candles had to be carried about the house because it was too expensive, time-consuming and dangerous to keep the upstairs rooms lit. Servants placed them in holders on the hall table for people to carry upstairs to light them to bed.

Even in the sitting-room quite well-to-do people did not usually burn more than two candles at a time. Miss Matty Jenkyns in *Cranford* could only afford to burn one, but she always had two set out. Throughout the evening she kept extinguishing one and lighting the other. That way she managed to keep them both the same length so that if a visitor called unexpectedly they could both be lit and it would look as though she had been burning both all evening.

But even two candles do not give off much light and it is surprising that women managed to do so much sewing, embroidery and knitting by their dim light. Sometimes, if they could not afford candles they worked by the light of the fire. That was called 'keeping blindman's holiday'.

Oil lamps involved as much work as candles. They had to be kept filled with oil and constantly cleaned. If they were not well cared for or handled properly they could be very dangerous. Many fires were caused by lighted oil lamps being knocked over.

A portable oil lamp

A gas 'globe light'

Ladies worried about the effect electric light might have on their complexions

In Victorian times many town houses began to use gas lighting, either from wall-brackets or from large cast-iron or brass 'gaseliers' hanging from the centre of the ceiling. But gas was usually only used in the main rooms – the rest of the house was still lit by candles or oil lamps.

Gas lighting had many drawbacks. Some people complained that it was noisy, smelly and inconsistent, and that it caused extra housework by giving off impurities that stained the wallpaper and ceilings. By Edwardian times, people who could afford to were turning to electricity. But many households had a long wait for this clean and trouble-free form of lighting. Some houses did not have it installed until the 1950s.

HAPPY THOUGHT.

The Electric Light, so favourable to Furniture, Wall Papers, Pictures, Screens, &c., is not always becoming to the Female Complexion. Light Japanese Sunshades will be found invaluable.

5 Making fires

Open fires of wood or coal caused a lot of work in the days when they were the only form of heating.

In the Middle Ages it was the tradition in many houses never to let the fire go out because there was no easy way of lighting it again. At night, to prevent the risk of setting the house on fire, the embers were covered with a brass or copper cover called a 'curfew' (from the French *couvre-feu*). In the morning the smouldering ashes were blown back to life with a pair of bellows. Smoke from the central hearth curled round the room causing eyes to smart, and depositing soot everywhere, before it found an escape hole.

Keeping warm in the Middle Ages

A single central fire had to heat a huge baronial hall

Above Two types of coal scuttles

Right Black-leading the grate. Note the long-handled brush hanging on the wall

Fireplaces, common by Tudor times, made rooms a little cleaner by taking most of the smoke away up the chimney. But they needed a lot of attention, particularly in the tall, three-storey houses popular in Georgian and early Victorian times.

Servants had to spend a lot of time lugging coal up all the steep flights of stairs from the cellar. Heavy as it was, they were not allowed to leave the coal scuttle in any of the rooms. They had to carry it back and forth from the cellar every time the fires needed building up. Not until later Victorian times, when servants were less plentiful, were they allowed to leave the scuttle by the hearth, or fill a special coal box which stood there.

Brass and copper coal scuttles had to be kept well polished. So did the fire-irons – shovel, poker, tongs and long-handled brush. Usually the poker belonging to the set was only for show and a plainer one was kept for actual use.

A brass curfew made in the 1650s

No. 906.
Pokerette.
Best Quality.   Polished Brass.   Steel Butt.
Horn Handle.
4/- each.

A pair of bellows

No. 909.
Scissor Tongs.
Best Quality.   Polished Brass.
5 – each.

Grates caused a lot of bother. Imagine rising early on a freezing cold winter morning and going downstairs to clean out a grate before there could be any heat in the house. In large houses maids had several to do. They carried cinder pails containing a sifter which allowed ash to fall through, but retained the cinders for use in the kitchen.

The maids had a special box containing a substance called 'black-lead' for painting on to the iron parts to keep them black, as well as brushes, cloths and leathers for polishing shiny bits. When they had cleaned out the grates they had to lay the fires using screwed-up paper, a few sticks and coal, and then coax them to life with a pair of bellows.

As though there wasn't enough to do cleaning grates and tending fires, Victorian women liked to show off their 'artistic skill' by dressing up their fireplaces. They draped the mantelpieces with pelmets of cloth and arranged ornaments on top. In summer, when no fires were lit, hiding the black hole was a great challenge. They filled the grate with a fine material called gauze and sprinkled artificial flowers on it, made 'aprons' of folded paper, or filled the hearth with plants.

Time-saving gas and oil heaters became available by the end of the nineteenth century. Electric ones did not start to compete until the 1930s. But they were expensive to run compared with coal fires so they did not become really popular until they became cheaper after the Second World War.

Even today many people feel the friendly flicker and crackle of the flames makes the extra work involved in keeping an open fire worthwhile. But usually they also have a gas or electric fire for instant heat on cold mornings.

Servants were not always skilful fire-tenders!

6 Home decorating

Until the nineteenth century many people counted themselves lucky to have four walls and a roof of any sort for shelter. They were too poor to fuss about whether the interiors of their homes were pleasing to the eye or not. They lived with walls of bare stone, wood or brick, covered with soot and grime from the cooking fire.

But the well-to-do could afford to be more particular. In medieval times they had their walls plastered with a mixture of lime, sand and hair and brightened with whitewash, or they had them covered and warmed with hangings or wooden panelling called 'wainscot'.

Wall hangings were popular with lords who owned several estates because when they moved from one to another, the servants could roll them up and move them, thus making one set of decorations do for several houses.

Decorations were always expensive. Though the very rich could afford to be lavish, the less well-off were constantly looking for cheaper ways of achieving a grand effect.

A woven tapestry from Flanders, used to keep out draughts and decorate bare walls

Oak wainscotting inlaid with holly and bog oak

In the fifteenth, sixteenth and seventeenth centuries a fine woven tapestry from Flanders was what a fashion-conscious housewife dreamed of hanging in her main room. But if she couldn't afford one, she had to settle for a substitute called a 'steyned cloth'. This was a large piece of coarse canvas or linen which had scenes or patterns painted on it in water colours.

Alternatively, if she were in no great hurry, she could show off her skill as a needlewoman by embroidering her own hangings in colourful and intricate designs.

In the eighteenth century one of the favourite sorts of wall decoration was smooth plaster work known as 'stucco', painted in a pastel shade with decorative plaster mouldings picked out in white or gold.

To whitewash a cottage

Put half a peck of lime into a tub; pour in some water by degrees, and stir well with a stick that is broad at one end. When the lime and water are well mixed and the thickness of mud, strain it through a sieve into a vessel, when it will settle to the bottom; skim off the little water that remains on top and, when you are going to use it, mix it up with cold water to the thickness of thin paint.

Stuccoed walls and ceiling at Osterley Park House

Stucco was costly to have done, but looked beautiful when the walls were clean and fresh. The lady of the house had to be constantly on her guard against clumsy servants who might not treat her stuccoed walls with the necessary amount of care.

Mrs Whatman was probably writing from bitter experience when she insisted that servants should always be taught to put away 'chairs, tables or anything that goes next a wall, with a hand behind it. For want of this trifling attention', she complained, 'great pieces are frequently knocked out of the stucco, and the backs of chairs, if bending, leave a mark on the wall'.

In 1738 Mrs Purefoy of Shalstone in Buckinghamshire paid £14 to have 373 metres of inside painting done to her house in London. This doesn't sound much by today's standards, but it was more than a year's wages for many people then.

Because the cost of professional interior decoration was so high, some people were tempted to have a go at it themselves, or get their servants to do it. But it wasn't a simple job. You couldn't go out and buy a tin of paint – you had to mix your own.

A fine example of plasterwork completed in the 1740s

In a book called *The Complete Housewife*, Mrs Eliza Smith gives people instructions on how to mix paints at home. One of her practical tips is to buy six earthenware chamber pots to mix them in. Another tip is to boil up certain types of ingredients out of doors 'for fear of endangering the house'!

Here is Mrs Smith's price list of raw materials for those prepared to risk having a go:

One cwt of red-lead	18–0	(90p)
One cwt of white-lead	£1–2–0	(£1.10p)
Linseed oil by the gallon	3–0	(15p)

Judging by those figures, the cost of home decorating then, as now, could be vastly reduced by do-it-yourself.

A Victorian sitting-room. This kind of very ornate wallpaper was popular during the second half of the 19th century

By the early nineteenth century a coating of home-made whitewash was the usual decoration for all rooms in cottages. Industrial workers in the Midlands and North used whitewash too, but they sometimes stencilled a coloured pattern on to it. In the Second World War, when wallpaper was scarce, householders who wanted patterns had to resort to decorating plain walls themselves in a similar way. 'Stippling' them with a piece of rag dipped into differently coloured paints was a popular method.

Wallpaper was used in the eighteenth century, but it was hand-made by craftsmen and therefore a luxury only the rich could afford.

It wasn't widely used until the middle of the nineteenth century when it began to be machine-made in large quantities, and cheaply enough for middle-class and more affluent working-class people to use it. They tended to favour rich dark colours and ornate designs, perhaps because these did not show the dirt from coal fires and candles, and oil or gas lights.

The papers of those days were not washable like many modern ones. Nevertheless, inventive Victorian housewives found ways of cleaning them.

To clean wallpaper
First blow off the dust with a good pair of bellows. Wipe lightly downward with two days' old bread cut into half quarters.

7 Preparing food

People used to spend a lot more time preparing food than we do today. Until the twentieth century it was impossible to buy vegetables chopped and ready-cooked in a tin or frozen into packs for the convenience of housewives in a hurry. Chickens weren't plump 'oven-ready' parcels of meat with polythene-wrapped innards. Nor were pork, beef and lamb butchered into family-sized joints bearing no resemblance to the animals they came from.

In a country kitchen vegetables came muddy from the kitchen garden; chickens came feathered and freshly killed from the backyard; and pigs' carcasses came whole, unbutchered, from the sty. A housewife had to know how to deal with them. She had to be able to turn them into meals immediately, and also to preserve and ration them, in order to feed the household through the winter months when fresh meat and vegetables were scarce.

Country housewives used mostly home-produced food. Goods that had to be bought, like salt, were bought in bulk two or three times a year.

Preparing a meal before convenience foods were invented was often a long job

To smoke bacon
Rub the fitches well with bran or fine saw-dust and hang them in the chimney, out of the way of rain, and not near enough the fire to melt. The smoke must be from wood, stubble or litter. A month's smoking should be enough.

Cutting up a pig's carcase

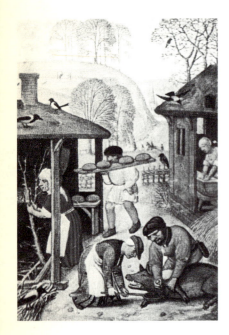

To prepare the blood for hog puddings
Save a quart or more of the blood and let it be stirred with salt until quite cold.
(If you have children, the recipe adds, let one of them do this!)

Town-dwellers had to buy more of their food, but they still bought in large quantities and prepared it all themselves.

What to do with a pig

The most common animal carcase a housewife found herself faced with was a pig's – usually the family pig's. Until well into the twentieth century, families kept a pig in a sty in the backyard and fattened it on kitchen scraps. In its lifetime they treated it with great care and even affection. But when the time came for the pig-sticker to kill it, they celebrated.

Pig-killing meant a feast of fresh meat. There was also meat to offer to friends and neighbours, to sell for cash, which usually bought new shoes, and to feed the family in the coming months. They couldn't afford to be sentimental or squeamish.

In those pre-refrigeration days the housewife had to work hard to make sure that none of the pig was wasted. She had to salt, smoke and pickle the meat to preserve it. She turned the fat into lard, made black puddings from the blood and brawn from the head. In fact, there was very little of 'Piggy' that a housewife, with time and effort, couldn't turn into a meal.

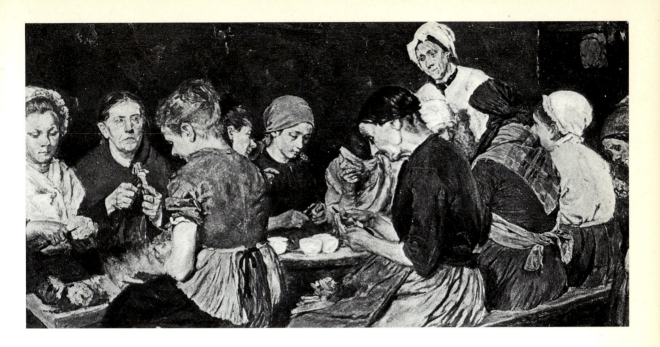

Making fresh fruit and vegetables into preserves

Pickling and preserving fruit and vegetables

For times when fresh fruit and vegetables were out of season, housewives had to do all their own pickling, preserving and drying. In the kitchen (or a room called the 'still-room' in large houses) the mistress and her maids dealt with piles of produce which had to be sliced, pared, topped and tailed. There were also pickling jars to scrub out and mixtures of vinegar and salt, or wine and sugar, to concoct.

They dealt with huge quantities at a time. A typical Elizabethan recipe began, 'Take 500 gerkins . . .' – enough to make a modern housewife, even with assistants, take fright!

Making butter and cheese

Country housewives made their own butter and cheese with the help of dairy maids. They had to rise as early as four o'clock in the morning to milk the cows. After making the butter and cheese they had to swill down the dairy and scrub all the utensils spotlessly clean.

Some well-to-do households, who preferred home-made cheese to bought, hired a cow for the summer months and it supplied them with enough cheese to last the whole year.

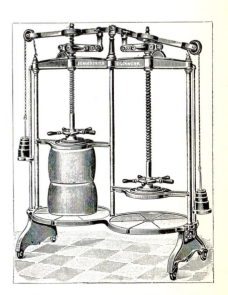

A cheese press

An old cider mill

Brewing

Tea was not widely drunk until the nineteenth century, and coffee and soft drinks not until the twentieth. Most people drank beer and ale with their meals, including breakfast. Even the children drank weak ale. Brewing was yet another job that housewives were commonly expected to do.

A housewife usually brewed her beer in autumn, making enough to last the whole year; but she had to brew ale more frequently – about once a month. Sometimes she made cider too, and wines from home-grown fruits and vegetables or wild plants like cowslips, nettles and elderberries gathered from the fields or hedgerows.

Baking bread

Until fairly recently poorer people lived mostly on bread, which they ate at every meal. It had to be baked several times a week in large batches.

In the Middle Ages very few housewives had their own oven for baking bread. They had to carry the dough to the baker's shop or to the lord of the manor's oven and pay to have it baked. In isolated cottages, where there was no oven nearby, they had to put the lumps of dough on the hot stones around the fire.

A bread oven built into the wall beside the chimney

THE CHEATING BAKER

In the Middle Ages, a baker who cheated his customers was dragged round the town on a sledge with a loaf of bread round his neck

By the sixteenth century many cottages had bread ovens built into the wall beside the chimney. But they weren't easy to use. A large pile of firewood had to be lit in the bottom, left to burn for two or three hours, and then raked aside before the bread could be put inside to bake in the stored-up heat.

Not all ovens were built into the cottages themselves. Some were a short distance away in a little building which they often shared with a 'copper' (boiler) for washing clothes. Housewives had to patter out across the yard in all weathers to use them.

Some poorer families, even though they had ovens, couldn't afford the fuel to heat them. It must have annoyed housewives very much to have to carry their dough and the family's Sunday dinner, often the only hot meal of the week, round to the baker's while their own ovens stood cold and empty.

By the end of the nineteenth century some housewives had been tempted to give up making their own dough, and had started buying bread ready-baked from roundsmen who delivered it daily. But many women preferred to keep on baking their own. They had to judge the oven's temperature by noting how long it took to char a piece of paper.

Modern facilities make the job of baking bread much easier. Home bread-baking is now on the increase again as part of a trend away from tasteless, commercially produced food. For those who simply want the enjoyment of bread fresh and hot from the oven without the bother of actually making it themselves, there are bread-mixes and even frozen doughs ready shaped to put straight in the oven. One couldn't have simpler bread-baking than that!

Delivering bread

8 Cooking and kitchen equipment

Cooking meals in large households used to occupy a great part of the day. Well-to-do people ate a lot of food by our standards and meals usually consisted of several courses. Preparing them and then tidying up afterwards kept a number of servants busy from six in the morning until late at night. The complicated recipes required an array of pots, dishes and moulds, as well as cooking aids like roasting spits and wall-ovens.

But for an ordinary cottage housewife cooking was not so complicated. In a book called *Lark Rise to Candleford*, Flora Thompson describes how cooking was done in the village of Lark Rise at the end of the nineteenth century.

> About four o'clock smoke would go up from the chimneys, as the fire was made up and the big iron boiler, or the three-legged pot, was slung on the hook of the chimney-chain. Everything was cooked in one utensil; the square of bacon, amounting to little more than a taste each; cabbage, or other green vegetables in one net, potato in another, and the roly-poly swathed in a cloth.

These methods of cooking had not changed since the Middle Ages.

The mistress of the house gives orders to her cook

Right Tasting a stew to see if it's cooked

Opposite A kitchen as it might have looked in Lark Rise

Dogs were often made to run inside a wheel to turn the spit. They were called turnspits

An early gas cooker dated 1859

Cooking was still being done over an open fire in some country areas at the time of the First World War. But, by then, most homes had at least a cast-iron cooking range. These had become common in town kitchens in Victorian times.

Though ranges made the task of cooking simpler, caring for them involved a lot of hard work. They had to be fed enormous quantities of coal and needed constant black-leading. But they were fairly economical, for coal was comparatively cheap. As well as producing heat for cooking, they warmed the room and sometimes boiled water – all at the same time.

Gas cookers for use in the home became available in about 1860. Even though they were much more efficient, they were rather slow in becoming popular because, unlike ranges, they didn't warm the room or heat water. But by the late 1920s they were being strongly recommended in housekeeping books; electric cookers were still having 'teething troubles' and oil cookers were dismissed as 'smelly'. Even so cast-iron ranges were still very popular in the 1920s and they continued to be used well into the 1950s.

Modern gas and electric cookers do almost everything automatically. If anyone had told a sixteenth-century housewife, as she scraped ash out of her wall-oven, or a Victorian housewife on her knees with a black-leading brush, that one day there would be ovens that would 'clean themselves', cook a meal while everybody was out for the day and have it ready for their return – or even cook a joint of meat in a matter of seconds, as micro-wave ovens do – they would never have believed it.

Kitchen cleanliness

In the sixteenth century a writer stressed the need for cleanliness in the kitchen. 'A housewife', he wrote, 'must be cleanly both in person and garments'. In Victorian times Mrs Beeton insisted that 'cleanliness is the most essential ingredient in the art of cooking; a dirty kitchen being a disgrace to both mistress and maid'.

But in those days it was impossible to keep a kitchen clean by our standards. Cooking done over open fires or on coal-burning ranges produced soot, ashes and smoke. In poorer homes the kitchen was also the living-room, so food was prepared and cooked in the midst of all the other family activities – not in special, hygienic surroundings. The pine or deal table on which most food was prepared couldn't be wiped over with soap and a cloth but had to be scrubbed clean.

Most old pictures of kitchens show a cat lurking near the fire – a reminder that kitchens, store-rooms and larders were infested by mice. In Mrs Beeton's day, suggestions in fashionable magazines for ridding houses of mice were almost as numerous as those for clearing beds of bugs.

The serious objection to poisoning rats and mice is that they die under the flooring, and behind the wainscotting, and so become a terrible nuisance. The trap, baited with nux vomica and oatmeal, is the best remedy. Any unusual noise will frighten away rats. A pistol or gun discharged occasionally near their holes, will in time drive them away.

9 Washing up

In the Middle Ages plates weren't washed up – they were eaten. Most people used 'trenchers', thick slices of four-day-old bread, as plates. When the meat was finished the trenchers were offered to the servants or thrown to the dogs. There were spoons to wash up, but no forks because they weren't in common use until the late seventeenth century. People used their fingers. They were expected to supply their own knives and clean them on a piece of bread.

Households in the Middle Ages owned platters, bowls and mugs of wood and perhaps a few dishes of pewter (a mixture of tin and lead). It wasn't until the sixteenth and seventeenth centuries that pewter came into common use.

With more dishes came the inconvenience of having to wash them. It wasn't easy without running water. A pail of water had to be carried from a well or the nearest fountain and specially boiled over the fire. Congealed fat was removed with a scouring of sand.

In the eighteenth century poorer people used wood and earthenware utensils for eating and drinking. The rich used pewter or silver, but for the new craze of tea drinking they bought a fine china tea service. The lady of the house often prized it so much she washed it up herself.

The commoner pewterware was left to a scullery maid to deal with. A lady named Hannah Glasse wrote down instructions for maids on how to clean pewter without scratching it and to make it as 'bright and fine as any silver'. It was done with a pail of wood ashes, half a pail of 'unslacked' lime and some soft water. This mixture was put into a large copper and the pewter plates, mugs and dishes were boiled in it.

Mrs Glasse also gave instructions on cleaning cooking pots and pans which became very black from being used over open fires. Generally they were made of iron, but sometimes of brass or copper. Whichever metal was used, they were so large and heavy to handle it is not surprising she needed to urge people not to neglect cleaning them. 'A whole family', she warns, 'died owing to verdigrease' (or 'verdigris', the greenish deposit which sometimes forms on copper when it isn't cleaned for a time).

A 17th-century pewter jug

Cooking pans, called skillets

Drinking tea from china cups, or 'dishes', became fashionable in the 18th century

A knife and fork with carved ivory handles

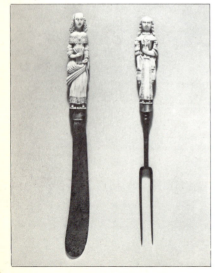

Hannah Glasse then advised her readers that 'This might be accustomned [prevented] by scouring the inside of the utensils with sand. If any scraping is required, use your nails.'

Cleaning table silver was a weekly job in wealthier homes. Some of the recipes for doing it seem so complicated it is surprising they were ever followed.

Instructions for washing china and earthenware in Victorian times show that methods were very similar to those of today. They were washed in plenty of warm soap and water, rinsed in a second bowl, then drained and wiped dry on linen tea-cloths. However the job was often not done in the warm atmosphere of the kitchen but in a cold, dismal little scullery adjoining it.

Cleaning knives and forks was a more difficult job then because the steel they were made of was not

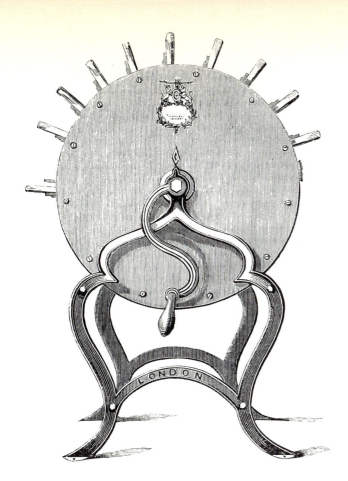

To boil plate (clean silver)
Take 12 gallons of water, or a quantity according to your plate in largeness or quantity; there must be water enough to cover it; put the water in a copper, or a large kettle; and when it boils put in half a pound of red argol, a pound of common salt, an ounce of rock-alum; first put your plate into a charcoal fire, and cover it till it is red hot; then throw it into your copper, and let it boil half an hour; then take it out, and wash it in cold fair water, and set it before the charcoal fire till it is very dry.

Left A rotary knife-cleaning machine

stainless. They were cleaned on a wooden board made of ash or deal, which was sometimes leather-covered, and stubborn stains were rubbed with cork or brickdust. Some households had a knife-cleaning machine.

In the 1920s housewives were being urged to buy stainless steel kitchen equipment if they could possibly afford it because the amount of work it saved 'had to be experienced to be believed'.

By the 1950s there was a new work-saver – the dishwasher. But there wasn't a mad rush to buy because, at first, they weren't very efficient. In the 1960s their performance improved and they became more popular, but even today most housewives still consider them far less essential than a washing-machine. This is because other equipment like non-stick baking tins, gaily-coloured polythene bowls and brushes and pleasant-smelling detergents, as well as efficient and fairly economical hot-water systems, all help to make washing up by hand far less dreary and arduous than it used to be.

One of the first attempts at making a dishwasher

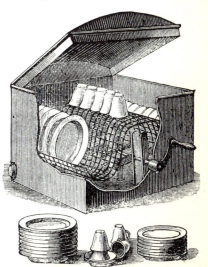

10 Making clothes

To us, clothing a family usually means a few visits to the shops to buy ready-made items. In the past, it meant sheer hard work. Until the nineteenth century country housewives often had not only to cut out and stitch every single garment by hand, but also to make the cloth itself.

The raw materials for making cloth were home-produced. Each year a husband would hand over to his wife a quantity of untreated flax, or hemp (for linen), and newly-sheared wool and expect her to turn it into cloth. She then had to transform it into clothes and other items, such as sheets and table-cloths, for the entire household.

Spinning wool in the Shetlands in the early 20th century. The woman on the left is using a 'card' to comb the wool before it's spun

A tailor's shop in the 18th century. Only the rich could afford to have clothes made for them

Most young girls, rich as well as poor, were taught to spin. Until the eighteenth century they used a distaff and spindle, but the introduction of the spinning-wheel speeded up the job quite a lot. Even so, they had to sit for long hours at their wheels to produce enough thread for all their needs.

Weaving was not usually the woman's job. It was left to a professional weaver who either collected the thread and took it to his own cottage to weave, or else stayed in the house and wove it on the house loom. Though she did not do the job herself, every good housewife was advised to have some knowledge of weaving so that she could keep an eye on his workmanship.

To die wooll blacke
You shall take two pound of galles (*oak apples*) **and bruise them, then take half as much of the best green coperas** (*iron sulphate*) **and boile them together in two gallons of running water, then shall you put your wooll therein and boile it, so done take it foorth and drie it.**

Preparing woollen thread for weaving clothes

Pieces of cloth straight from the weaver were not ready for cutting out. If they were linen they still had to be bleached, or if wool, dyed. Housewives were not only expected to know how to do that too, they even had to concoct the dyes and bleaches themselves. The usual way of bleaching linen was by soaking it in buttermilk and spreading it out in the sun to dry. Dyes had to be made by boiling up berries, bark and roots which the women searched for in the surrounding countryside.

Up to the eighteenth century, outer clothing for everyday wear was usually made at home. Even stockings were hand knitted. The rich had special clothes made by a tailor, but these were still hand-stitched.

A writer of the late eighteenth century tells us how rare tailor-made items were. In the north of England, where plenty of sheep were kept, he claims that almost every article people wore, apart from shoes and hats, was made at home. There were many respectable people, he wrote, who 'never wore a bought pair of stockings, coat, nor waistcoat, in their lives; and, within these twenty years, a coat bought at a shop was considered as a mark of extravagance and pride'.

In the south of England, where fewer people kept sheep, housewives bought their cloth from shops or from travelling pedlars, if they could afford to. But even the cheapest cloth was beyond the means of a poor housewife. Her family never had new clothes. She had to rely on buying them second-hand from old-clothes dealers. Fortunately, the thick woollen clothes of those days were very hard wearing and, by means of mending, patching and even unpicking the seams and turning the clothes inside out, she made them last.

In the latter half of the nineteenth century, when machines had made more off-the-peg clothes available, country housewives still had to rely on second-hand outer garments. In *Lark Rise to Candleford,* Flora Thompson tells us how in Lark Rise they had to depend on 'daughters and sisters, and aunts away in service, who all sent parcels, not only of their own clothes, but also of those they could beg from their mistresses'. These, she explains, 'were worn and altered and dyed and turned and alternately patched and darned as long as the threads held together'.

Buying cloth from a pedlar

The original Singer sewing machine, made in 1854

The girls of Lark Rise made their underwear at school from hard-wearing material supplied by the rector and his wife – 'harsh but strong flannel petticoats and worsted stockings that would stand up with no legs in them'!

But for middle-class and more prosperous working-class housewives, the mid-nineteenth century brought two great boons. One was the increase of ready-to-wear clothes, made possible by the introduction of synthetic fabrics. The other was the invention, by an American named Isaac Singer, of a machine to do all the laborious stitching for them. Sewing-machines saved housewives hours of time and effort. In the 1860s they were being advertised at between £5 and £10 each.

In this 1898 advertisement the pattern for each costume was sent free with every purchase

Another helpful innovation was paper patterns, offered by magazines such as *The Young Ladies Journal* and *The English Women's Domestic Magazine*. In the 1860s a pattern for a dress cost about 25p, postage included. But it is heartening to learn that then, as now, not every woman was skilled enough to use a paper pattern correctly. 'If you undertake at all to offer patterns to the public in your *English Women's Domestic Magazine*, wrote an angry correspondent named Sophia Anderson to the letters column in 1862, 'you should offer *correct* ones .... I should like to know how it would be possible to make a little boy's jacket ... such as you depicted in this month's number? There is no place for the arm-hole.' The pattern *was* correct and the editor printed such a scornful reply that poor Sophia must have been left very red-faced.

Women of today who, like Sophia Anderson, have doubtful dress-making skills, must be thankful to be living in the twentieth century with shops and mail-order firms offering a wide choice of factory-produced clothes at prices to suit every pocket.

Ready-to-wear clothes became more widely available from the 1850s

59

11 Servantless homes

All the vast amount of work that had to be done in the past meant it was impossible to run any but the simplest home without servants.

The rich employed dozens and by Victorian times the better-off working classes had at least one girl to help with the heavy work. Servants were expected to work from six in the morning until late at night, doing all the drudgery of the house for very little pay. At the end of the day they slept in comfortless beds, often in the attic or, in the case of men servants, in the cellar.

Servants had good cause to complain. But mistresses did their share of complaining too. The difficulties of finding, keeping, paying and controlling a staff of often unreliable servants seem to have given them constant headaches. However, as one Victorian writer pointed out, 'The double or treble of what they are paid would not compensate us for the discomfort of having to work for ourselves . . . .'

After the First World War mistresses discovered the truth of that warning. More jobs became available in shops and offices, and women were attracted away from domestic service.

Employers began to learn what it was like to do their own chores, and without servants their attitude to housework soon changed. They discovered that all the old laborious methods of doing housework were impossible single-handed. They began to demand smaller, more compact, labour-saving houses.

Most housewives eventually got, or are getting fitted kitchens, electric lights, gas and electric cookers and fires, vinyl floor and wall coverings, plastic and formica-topped surfaces, vacuum-cleaners, washing-machines and all the other devices that make modern housework so much easier.

An expensively fitted 20th-century kitchen

A Dorset farm labourer's cottage in 1846

All these improvements make it possible for a woman not only to run her home without help, but to do a job outside the home too if she wants. Working-class women had often been forced by poverty to go out to work. Easier housework means all classes of women can now do so by choice, knowing they are not neglecting their homes.

Working wives have in their turn brought a change in men's attitude to housework in modern times. In Victoria's reign it was said that men's business at home was to make work for others, not do it themselves. Nowadays they usually expect to do their share.

So if ever you should find yourself longing for life as it was, in the days when a household was largely self-sufficient, just remember what a lot of hard work went into providing a hearth-rug, glowing fire, flickering candles, and those slices of bread dangling on a toasting fork.

Books for further reading

Allen, Eleanor, *Wash and Brush Up,* A & C Black

Baker, Margaret, *Food and Cooking,* A & C Black

Mrs Beeton's Book of Household Management (this includes many Victorian recipes and tips on housekeeping, from making beds to black-leading)

Ellacott, S. E., *The Story of the Kitchen,* Methuen

Harrison, Molly, *The Kitchen in History,* Osprey

Lofts, Norah, *Domestic Life in England,* Weidenfeld & Nicolson (covers the period from the Norman Conquest to the present day)

Thompson, Flora, *Lark Rise to Candleford,* OUP, Penguin (an autobiography with lots of interesting information on the home life of cottage dwellers in late Victorian times)

Acknowledgments

The author and publishers are grateful to the following for permission to reproduce photographs:

Ardea 24; Batsford 49; British Gas Corporation 61; Camera Press 4a; Cooper-Bridgeman Library 7, 8b, 11, 18, 23, 25, 27a, 33b, 34c, 37, 48a, 48b, 51a, 51b, 52, 55; Greater London Council 14; Mansell Collection 4b, 21a, 33a, 35b, 41, 42a, 42b, 43a, 45a, 45b, 46a, 46b, 53a, 54, 56; Mary Evans Picture Library 13a, 15a, 15b, 16b, 19a, 21b, 21c, 26, 27b, 29a, 30b, 31a, 31b, 32a, 32b, 34a, 34b, 35a, 40, 43b, 44a, 53b, 57, 59a, 59b; John Murray (Publishers), Ltd 20; Museum of English Rural Life 5, 19b, 44b; National Trust 8a, 12, 17, 36, 38, 39, 47; *Punch* 16a; Radio Times Hulton Picture Library 29b, 30a, 58; Welsh Folk Museum 28.

Index

anti-macassars 21

baking 44, 45
bed-bugs 25, 26, 49
Beeton, Mrs 26, 49
bellows 17, 33, 35, 40
black-lead 34, 35, 40
bleaches 56
brewing 44
brooms 8, 9, 10, 13, 15, 16
brushes 9, 10, 15, 18, 21, 34, 35, 48
bullocks' blood 5
butter-making 43

candles 30, 31, 62
candle-making 4, 28, 29
candlesticks 30
carpets 8, 11, 15
carpet sweeper 13, 16
castles 6, 29, 32, 40
cellar 34, 60
chamber pots 26, 39
cheese-making 43
Chippendale, Thomas 17, 18
coal box 34
coal scuttle 34
cooking range 48, 49
Crusades, 11
curfew 33, 34

detergents 53
dish-washing machine 53
dress-making 56, 59
druggets 12, 15
dry-rubbing 9
dust sheets 10, 17, 20
duvets 27

Edwardian times 32
electric appliances:
  blankets 27
  cookers 48, 61
  floor-polishers 5, 16
  heaters 35
  lights 32, 61

electricity 28, 32
Elizabeth I 7, 11
Erasmus 7

feather beds 23, 24
fires 4, 33, 35, 46
fleas 6
floor cloth 14
foot-scraper 14
furniture polish 19, 20

gas appliances:
  cookers 48, 61
  heaters 35
  lighting 19, 32, 40
gaselier 31, 32
Gaskell, Mrs 13, 20
Georgian times 34
Glasse, Mrs 51
grates 34, 35
grease stains 30

hens 23, 24
herbs 7
hot-water bottles 27

knife-cleaning 52, 53

ladies magazines 20, 25, 49, 59
linoleum 14

maids 10, 15, 17, 21, 26, 27, 35, 43, 49, 51
mail-order 59
marble floors 12, 14
mops 10

oil appliances:
  heaters 35
  lamps 28, 31, 32
  lighting 19, 30, 40
ornaments 17, 19, 20, 35

pans 51
paper patterns 59
pickling 43

pictures 17, 20
pigs 41, 42
plague 7
preserving 43
Purefoy, Mrs 38

rushes 5, 6, 8, 11, 29
rush lights 29, 30
rush matting 8
Rowland's Macassar Oil 21

scrubbing brush 9
servants 6, 8, 16, 20, 22, 25, 30, 31, 34–36, 46, 60, 61
sewing machine 58
shutters 19
Singer, Isaac 58
Smith, Eliza 39
snuffers 29, 30
stucco 37, 38
sweeping 10, 13

tapestries 36, 37
tea-leaves 10, 13
tenterhooks 11
Thompson, Flora 46, 57
Tudor times 7, 8, 22, 34

underwear 58, 59

Venetian blinds 9, 18
Victorians 20, 21, 24, 26, 27, 32, 34, 35, 40, 49, 52, 60, 62
vacuum-cleaners 5, 15, 16, 61

wages 8, 10, 38
wainscot 36, 37, 49
wall-hangings 36
wallpaper 32, 40
warming pans 27
washing-machines 61
weaving 55, 56
Whatman, Mrs 12, 13, 18, 19, 24, 30, 38
whitewash 36, 38, 40
window-cleaning 20, 21

64